THE Road to Oz

TWISTS, TURNS, BUMPS, AND TRIUMPHS IN THE LIFE OF L. FRANK BAUM

BY KATHLEEN KRULL ILLUSTRATED BY KEVIN HAWKES

ALFRED A. KNOPF NEW YORK

To Janet Schulman, with thanks

—K.K.

To Katie and Logan

Many thanks to Jessica Thomas and Deanna Gouzie

at the Baxter Memorial Library

—K.H.

THIS IS A BORZOI BOOK PUBLISHED BY ALFRED A. KNOPF

Text copyright © 2008 by Kathleen Krull
Illustrations copyright © 2008 by Kevin Hawkes

All rights reserved. Published in the United States by Alfred A. Knopf, an imprint of
Random House Children's Books, a division of Random House, Inc., New York.

Knopf, Borzoi Books, and the colophon are registered trademarks of Random House, Inc.

Visit us on the Web! www.randomhouse.com/kids

Educators and librarians, for a variety of teaching tools, visit us at
www.randomhouse.com/teachers

Library of Congress Cataloging-in-Publication Data
Krull, Kathleen.
The road to Oz : twists, turns, bumps, and triumphs in the life of L. Frank Baum / by
Kathleen Krull ; illustrated by Kevin Hawkes. — 1st ed.
p. cm.
ISBN 978-0-375-83216-1 (trade) — ISBN 978-0-375-93216-8 (lib. bdg.)
1. Baum, L. Frank (Lyman Frank), 1856–1919—Juvenile literature. 2. Authors, American—
20th century—Biography—Juvenile literature. I. Hawkes, Kevin, ill. II. Title.
PS3503.A923Z726 2008
813'.4—dc22
[B]
2007041526

The text of this book is set in 14-point Goudy.
The illustrations in this book were created using India ink and acrylic on paper.

MANUFACTURED IN CHINA
September 2008
10 9 8 7 6 5 4 3 2 1

First Edition

Every road leads somewhere, or there wouldn't be any road.
—*The Road to Oz* by L. Frank Baum

Once upon a time, there was no Dorothy from Kansas and her little dog, Toto. There was no tornado that whirled them to a magic world named Oz. No Good Witch who kissed Dorothy's forehead and left a lasting, protective mark. No talking Scarecrow, Tin Woodman, Cowardly Lion. No flying monkeys, or sleepy field of poppies. No Wizard who turned out to be a humbug. No yellow brick road to the Emerald City. . . .

Someone had to make it all up.

thin boy darted along a path, a thick book in his hands. This white gravel path was just one of many that curled over the acres of his lawn.

It was 1860s America, rural New York to be exact, and Lyman Frank Baum's family was rich.

Rosebushes dotted their emerald-green front yard. Hundreds of rosebushes in glimmering-jewel colors. In their honor, the Baums called their estate Rose Lawn. And those white paths—like miniature roads made of diamonds—were a map to somewhere . . . anywhere . . . wherever the boy could imagine.

Frank grew up pampered, some might say spoiled.

(No one dared call him Lyman—who *wouldn't* hate that name?)

Tutors came from England to teach him at home. He had plenty of brothers and sisters to play with and a best friend in his younger brother Harry. Their mother and father—a businessman—gave them whatever they wanted.

He was frail and gentle, a reader who took the white paths around Rose Lawn to find places to curl up with a book. He memorized words by Shakespeare, Dickens, and other classic British authors.

When he was twelve, his parents sent him away to military school. But they brought him back home when he hated it.

He spent vast amounts of time daydreaming, making things up. Everything was alive to him, even objects. Those scarecrows out in the farms and fields around Rose Lawn—at night he dreamed they were chasing him.

Writing always came easily to Frank. When he was fourteen, his father bought him his own printing press. Frank and Harry wrote and printed the *Rose Lawn Home Journal*, a monthly newspaper about Baum family life.

How delicious it was to play with words! Especially in one's very own newspaper. To polish words into poems, to make up stories, to entertain with riddles, to poke fun with mocking "news items."

Oh, the days were always too short for all Frank wanted to do. In his teens, he attempted his first novel. When he got obsessed with stamp collecting, he started up a magazine— *The Stamp Collector*—describing all the latest news.

At age eighteen, he tried to focus on just one thing he could do as a career.

(But it was so hard to decide. . . .)

Frank chose a life on the stage. He had become enthralled by performers traveling around New York. The theater was an enchanting world of pure make-believe. It was also a career full of risks.

One company allowed him to join, only if he brought along five trunks of wigs and costumes, worth thousands of dollars. One by one, the other actors "borrowed" an expensive costume. But Frank never got any roles.

So he founded his own company. He wrote his own dramas and played all the lead roles. His troupe traveled to tiny towns, at times performing on a "stage" that was merely pieces of wood set on top of sawhorses.

One night, as Hamlet, Frank accidentally moved a plank. Suddenly the actor playing a ghost vanished below. The audience howled, thinking this was deliberate, and made them enact the absurd maneuver over and over.

(Not exactly the glamorous life he had envisioned.)

He did have one hit—an Irish melodrama he wrote and starred in, called *The Maid of Arran*. But his bookkeeper stole the money. Then a fire destroyed all his props.

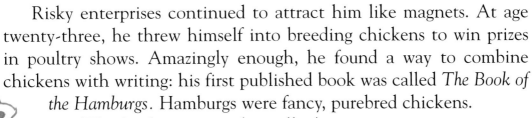

Risky enterprises continued to attract him like magnets. At age twenty-three, he threw himself into breeding chickens to win prizes in poultry shows. Amazingly enough, he found a way to combine chickens with writing: his first published book was called *The Book of the Hamburgs*. Hamburgs were fancy, purebred chickens.

(The book was not a bestseller.)

For a while he was a traveling salesman, selling oil for lubrication and kerosene lamps. Not much to write about. Plus, one day he came back to his office to find his head clerk dead—he had shot himself after gambling away all Frank's earnings.

Bad luck, bad planning, too much ambition, too much risk . . .

("Will he ever amount to anything?" some people whispered.)

Frank knew he wasn't a failure.

(He was fairly sure.)

His greatest skill, perhaps, was for family life.

At age twenty-six, he married his true love. Maud Gage was the daughter of an important fighter for women's right to vote. Fondly combining writing with Maud, he wrote articles about how to be a good husband.

(As if this wasn't enough, he bought her an expensive box of candy every single week.)

And he devoted himself to their four sons. He spent hours with each baby, romping on the floor, singing lullabies. Family dinners were a fest of jokes, songs, trivia contests.

In the summer, they bicycled to the park for picnics and concerts. In the winter, a husky pulled the boys around on sleds. One son loved making gadgets, and Frank allowed him to drill holes and install battery-operated contraptions anywhere he liked.

Each Fourth of July, their yard exploded with skyrockets and pinwheels.

(Where did the fireworks come from? Frank sold them on the side.)

The local doctor, if he heard any yelling in the neighborhood, would automatically head to the Baums'.

"If I had my way," one of his sons remembered Frank saying, "I would always have a young child in the house."

("I wouldn't," said Maud.)

In the evenings, Frank told bedtime stories—Mother Goose, fairy tales. Storytelling—now, *this* was the role of a lifetime.

Night after night, he noticed how action kept the boys alert, unexpected dangers and whirling escapes. To frighten was tempting, but Frank dreaded the thought of giving a child nightmares, so he never got too bloodcurdling. Mocking humor worked, as did a clear way of telling that wasted no words. The child-heroes should be resourceful, the grown-ups a bit dim.

There were no books like this, so he made things up. The Baum boys began bringing friends home in the evening.

(Was it Frank's stories? Or the popcorn, taffy, and ice cream he served up with them?)

Frank also took note of what his listeners *didn't* like. Romances between princes and princesses made them itch. No lecturing. They *hated* being talked down to. Nothing cute, or what he called "goody-goody." Long descriptions of nature put them to sleep, as did fairy tales where girls were always being rescued.

Gradually, he discovered what worked best—taking his audience to a new universe, full of marvels and details.

By now he was telling stories to fourteen, fifteen children at a time.

But still he had to earn a living. So, like many another go-getter of his day, he went west. In what later became South Dakota, he opened a store in a gray new frontier town. Aberdeen's unpaved Main Street now had Baum's Bazaar to sell games, fancy china, crafts from around the world, and lots of toys.

(He juggled writing with running a store by printing up clever verses in praise of his wares.)

He organized baseball teams so he could sell his balls and bats, but then didn't pay enough attention to the store during baseball season. He advertised 600 items, and they didn't always arrive. Worst of all was the drought, sucking life out of the farms. No one bought his umbrellas from Japan, or Gunther's Celebrated Chicago Candies.

He rejected his mother's offers to help. "I shall *somehow* manage to provide for those dependent on me," he said.

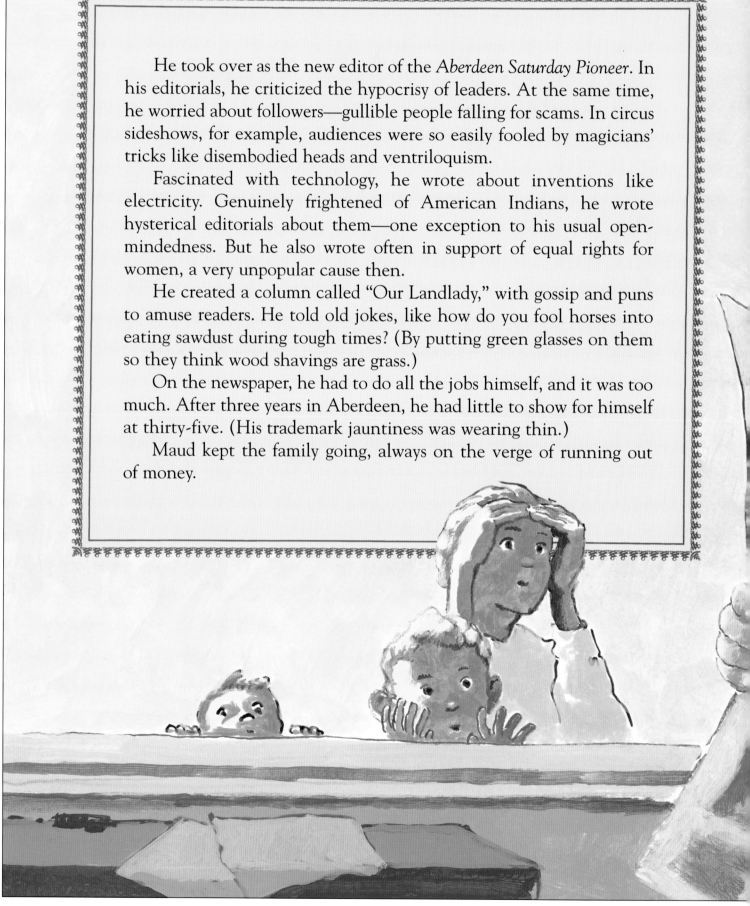

He took over as the new editor of the *Aberdeen Saturday Pioneer*. In his editorials, he criticized the hypocrisy of leaders. At the same time, he worried about followers—gullible people falling for scams. In circus sideshows, for example, audiences were so easily fooled by magicians' tricks like disembodied heads and ventriloquism.

Fascinated with technology, he wrote about inventions like electricity. Genuinely frightened of American Indians, he wrote hysterical editorials about them—one exception to his usual open-mindedness. But he also wrote often in support of equal rights for women, a very unpopular cause then.

He created a column called "Our Landlady," with gossip and puns to amuse readers. He told old jokes, like how do you fool horses into eating sawdust during tough times? (By putting green glasses on them so they think wood shavings are grass.)

On the newspaper, he had to do all the jobs himself, and it was too much. After three years in Aberdeen, he had little to show for himself at thirty-five. (His trademark jauntiness was wearing thin.)

Maud kept the family going, always on the verge of running out of money.

Frank still loved newspaper writing. He just needed a bigger city, with bigger papers. He moved to Chicago, where the only newspaper jobs he could get didn't pay enough to support the family. But they had moved just in time for the 1893 World's Fair, the largest and most thrilling one ever. A waterfront area in Chicago was set aside for the fair and named the White City. Glittering with tiny electric lights, it had miles of enchanting buildings showcasing the latest wonders in technology. And in fun, like the Ferris wheel.

No one who saw Chicago's White City ever forgot it. The Baums visited often.

(Almost as many times as they went to baseball games.)

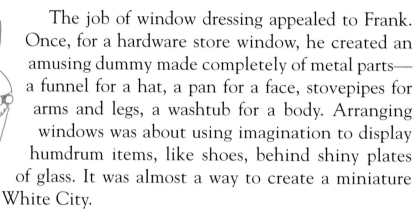

The job of window dressing appealed to Frank. Once, for a hardware store window, he created an amusing dummy made completely of metal parts— a funnel for a hat, a pan for a face, stovepipes for arms and legs, a washtub for a body. Arranging windows was about using imagination to display humdrum items, like shoes, behind shiny plates of glass. It was almost a way to create a miniature White City.

So he wrote a book, *The Art of Decorating Dry Goods Windows and Interiors*.

(This wasn't a bestseller, either.)

He tried being a traveling salesman for fancy dishes. At the Chicago Public Library, he read up on fine china. In each city, he would pack and unpack hundreds of fragile pieces. Being away from his family distressed him.

But while passing the time in bleak hotels or train stations, he wrote on the backs of envelopes and bits of paper. He came up with rhymes suitable for greeting card companies. He bought a printing press and printed a little book of his own verse, called *By the Candelabra's Glare*.

(Carrying on the family tradition, he gave the press to his sons, so they could print their own Baum newspaper.)

Finally it dawned on Frank that he could be writing down those bedtime fantasies he told the children.

(Actually, his mother-in-law was the one who pointed this out.)

He threw himself into creating original, modern American fairy tales. His house in Chicago might have lacked running water, but he did have a den of his own. After everyone had gone to bed, he'd curl up in a cozy chair, chain-smoking cigars, writing neatly in pencil, filling his file cabinet with ideas.

It took forever to find a publisher for *Adventures in Phunnyland*, his first book of fairy tales. But he remained undaunted, for seven long years.

(Though he kept a sad little book of rejections from publishers he called his Record of Failure.)

For a while, Frank had been pouring his powers of imagination into one big story. It was called "The Emerald City"—a sort of green version of Chicago's White City. It starred a resourceful Kansas girl and her little dog, Toto. They were on a strange road in a strange land: "The road to the City of Emeralds is paved with yellow brick, so you cannot miss it." In this land, everything is green (thanks to green glasses) and anything is possible. The girl marvels at a non-scary scarecrow, a man made of tin parts, a cowardly lion, a wizard who is really a fake, women who are all-powerful. . . .

Frank's young neighbors got to hear what he was working on. Now he was calling it "From Kansas to Fairyland"—from a gray Western state to a land full of rainbows.

One evening a girl asked him where these creatures lived. Baum liked to say that his glance happened to fall on his file cabinet: two drawers labeled A–N and O–Z.

"Oz!" was his reply.

The Wonderful Wizard of Oz finally appeared in 1900. Frank dedicated it to Maud, "my good friend and comrade."

(He might have said "patient" instead of "good.")

He had worked with an artist, William Wallace Denslow, who created twenty-four brilliant paintings of Oz. The two men paid part of the cost of publishing the book. It was such a big risk—a beautifully illustrated, original American novel written to amuse children. There was nothing else like it.

Frank's first clue about how his risk would pay off came near Christmas. The Baums were out of money again. Maud insisted he stop by his publisher's office to ask for some—even $100 would be a help.

So he did. The publisher wrote him a check, and he stuck it in his pocket without looking at it. Back at home, Maud was ironing shirts. The legend is that she asked for the money, then dropped the iron and burned a hole in a shirt.

(The check was for several thousand dollars.)

That Christmas season, Frank, at age forty-four, was the author of the bestselling children's book. Everyone wanted to journey to Oz.

The Baums bought their first telephone and finally got electricity. In an early Model T Ford, they began traveling all over, especially to spots in southern California, like the Hotel del Coronado, a magical miniature city near San Diego.

(Maud stayed in charge of the money.)

Frank Baum journeyed on for another nineteen years.

Once again, he and his family were rich. They lived in a mansion where elaborate white paths curled around lawns, flowers, and orange trees—the estate, called Ozcot, was in Hollywood. He kept forty birds, numerous goldfish, and a flock of chickens—Rhode Island Reds. Every day he tended to his enormous garden of award-winning flowers.

He built the house with an inheritance from his mother-in-law—because his money problems never went away.

(Too many risks.)

But children visited Ozcot often, sometimes in large groups from schools. In his garden, over glasses of lemonade, Frank would tell stories by the hour. He was on the right road.

(At last.)

STORYTELLER'S NOTE

In 1900, Lyman Frank Baum published *The Wonderful Wizard of Oz,* one of the best-loved creations in all of children's literature. At a time when books for the young were lectures in disguise, *Oz* was the Harry Potter of its day—a sensation. It is estimated that most American children have seen the famous movie (made from the book in 1939) at least once.

And yet Baum's life story is not well known. He was born on May 15, 1856, near Syracuse, New York. He tried many different careers on his long, curly road to success. To everything he did, he brought charm, style, a sense of humor, imagination. If any of his business ventures had gone well, Baum would be little known today. But they didn't.

Fan mail for *The Wonderful Wizard of Oz* convinced him to stay on the yellow brick road. "If I am to do any good in the world, my highest ambition will be to make children happy," he declared. He hadn't thought of the book as the start of a series, but its fans pleaded. He went on to write thirteen more Oz books, and more than seventy children's books in all. He wrote warm letters back to his fans, and sometimes even used their suggestions in his stories.

Oddly enough, he made much more money from a musical based on *Oz* than he did from the book. The musical charmed audiences for nine years. It was such a success that he kept trying to repeat it with other stage projects, not as successfully. Still, Baum dreamed on. With vaudeville in vogue, he toured with his "Fairylogue and Radio-Plays," an extravaganza starring himself. The play drained him financially, and in 1911 he had to declare bankruptcy.

The quality of his books was uneven, in part because he was keeping his eye on what would work onstage. His heroes were almost always self-reliant girls. One of his biggest influences was his mother-in-law, Matilda Joslyn Gage, who helped Elizabeth Cady Stanton and Susan B. Anthony found the National Woman Suffrage Association.

Baum finished the last two Oz books in bed as his heart was failing. After making notes for the fifteenth, he slipped into a coma. Other writers continued the series after his death on May 6, 1919, at age sixty-two.

Always his goal was to stimulate daydreams. "The imaginative child," he wrote, "will become the imaginative man or woman most apt to create, to invent, and therefore to foster civilization."

SOURCES

Baum, L. Frank. *Our Landlady*, edited by Nancy Tystad Koupal. Lincoln: University of Nebraska Press, 1996.

Glassman, Peter, ed. *Oz: The Hundredth Anniversary Celebration*. New York: HarperCollins, 2000.

Hearn, Michael Patrick, ed. *The Annotated Wizard of Oz*. New York: Norton, 2000.

Rogers, Katharine M. *L. Frank Baum, Creator of Oz: A Biography*. New York: St. Martin's, 2002.

L. FRANK BAUM'S OZ BOOKS

Some of the titles listed below include descriptive subtitles written by L. Frank Baum.

The Wonderful Wizard of Oz (1900)

The Marvelous Land of Oz: *A Sequel to The Wizard of Oz, Being an Account of the Further Adventures of the Scarecrow and Tin Woodman and also the Strange Experiences of the Highly Magnified Woggle-Bug, Jack Pumpkin-head, the Animated Saw-Horse and the Gump* (1904)

Ozma of Oz: *A Record of Her Adventures with Dorothy Gale of Kansas, the Yellow Hen, the Scarecrow, the Tin Woodman, Tiktok, the Cowardly Lion and the Hungry Tiger; Besides Other Good People too Numerous to Mention Faithfully Recorded Herein* (1907)

Dorothy and the Wizard in Oz: *A faithful record of their amazing adventures in an underground world; and how with the aid of their friends Zeb Hugson, Eureka the Kitten, and Jim the Cab-Horse, they finally reached the wonderful land of Oz* (1908)

The Road to Oz: *In which is related how Dorothy Gale of Kansas, The Shaggy Man, Button Bright, and Polychrome the Rainbow's Daughter met on an Enchanted Road and followed it all the way to the Marvelous Land of Oz* (1909)

The Emerald City of Oz (1910)

The Patchwork Girl of Oz (1913)

Tik-Tok of Oz (1914)

The Scarecrow of Oz (1915)

Rinkitink in Oz: *Wherein is recorded the Perilous Quest of Prince Inga of Pingaree and King Rinkitink in the Magical Isles that lie beyond the Borderland of Oz* (1916)

The Lost Princess of Oz (1917)

The Tin Woodman of Oz: *A Faithful Story of the Astonishing Adventure Undertaken by the Tin Woodman, assisted by Woot the Wanderer, the Scarecrow of Oz, and Polychrome, the Rainbow's Daughter* (1918)

The Magic of Oz: *A Faithful Record of the Remarkable Adventures of Dorothy and Trot and the Wizard of Oz, together with the Cowardly Lion, the Hungry Tiger and Cap'n Bill, in their successful search for a Magical and Beautiful Birthday Present for Princess Ozma of Oz* (1919)

Glinda of Oz: *In which are related the exciting experiences of Princess Ozma of Oz, and Dorothy, in their hazardous journey to the home of the Flatheads, and to the Magic Isle of the Skeezers, and how they were rescued from dire peril by the sorcery of Glinda the Good* (1920)